# The gods Among Us

**Also by Dr. Gwynn**

Easter–Not What You Think

Chrislam – What Communion Hath Light With Darkness?

Conflict – Christianity's Love vs. Islam's Submission

The President Was a Good Man

Anything for Acceptance

Healing – The Children's Bread

Created to Live!

# The gods Among Us

## Dr. Murl Edward Gwynn

Published by MEG Enterprises Publications
PO Box 2165
Reidsville, GA 30453
(912) 557-6507
meg@kencable.net
www.murlgwynn.com
www.megenterprises.org

Unless otherwise identified, Scripture quotations are from
the Holy Bible New International Version, copyright ©
1973, 1978, 1984 by International Bible Society.
Zondervan Publishing House. Used by permission.

Scripture quotations marked KJV are from the King James
Version of the Bible.

International Standard Book Number: 978-0-9711766-7-6

Printed in the U.S.A

# TABLE OF CONTENTS

# *ACKNOWLEDGMENTS*

Ruth

That God sent His Son!

# *PREFACE*

It never ceases to amaze me how far we have gotten away from a once firm conviction to never compromise when it comes to God's word and obedience to it.

Holy Scripture, from the Old Testament and all through the New Testament, warns God's children of deviating from His will and commands. God's warnings are not to keep a people in line with a dictatorial ruler or stern potentate, but to insure that the objects of His love remain pure, healthy, and fit in a corrupt and sin infested world. Mankind is the object of God's love!

God warns us to not worship false gods or to align ourselves with anything that comes from Satan or other dark and contrary beings. God goes as far as to say that He will hold every person accountable for their beliefs, actions, and thoughts, even in ignorance. In other words, our ignorance is no excuse once we are informed of truth.

Many Christians, in solid believing churches, observe the resurrection of Jesus, call it Easter, and celebrate it with eggs, bunnies, and the trappings associated with Easter. Most know that even the word Easter is the modern name for Astrate, a false goddess, which in ancient times was worshipped using sexual and fertility rites. It doesn't seem to matter that we shouldn't have anything to do with even mentioning the name Easter. Some even acknowledge that they know it is wrong, but still practice the egg hunts, bunnies, and bunny cakes. I am amazed!

Also, many Christians, dabble with items such as horoscopes, numerology, figurines, good luck charms, and other items that are associated with powers of darkness. In most cases, however, I believe they do it in ignorance. Because of the association with powers of darkness, whether in ignorance or not, many believers are sick in body, soul, and spirit.

I must add here, by no means am I blaming, judging, or condemning anyone. I have my own weaknesses! I am, however, trying to help the Church realize a truth, that I think will free us in many areas if we will respond according to the will of God.

It is my desire that the information in this book will help us cast off those things that are against God's will and often pulls us down and away from the best God has for us.

I believe we bind God's hands from bringing the best to us, which is His desire. I believe in our ignorance we fail to realize the best, when in reality we only realize portion. God wants to give us the maximum but can't, and we scrape to receive minimum.

It is my desire to help you, reader, to cast off all those things that keep you from realizing God's best. If we will truly obey God and His word, without compromising anything, I am convinced we will be the glorious Church He intended us to be.

# 1

# Belief

It makes all the difference in the world as
to what comes into our life and what we permit
into it. We permit everything into our lives either
by omission or commission. Omission[1] can
either be an understood omitting of truth,
refusing to respond to understood directions, or

---

[1] Omission = 1:something neglected or left undone, 2: the act of
omitting : the state of being omitted.

out-right rebellion to truth. Commission[2] is the willful consent, acted upon, either in word or deed, which brings about a desired result. When it comes to God's word and obedience, omission can result in spiritual darkness, death, or disease. On the other hand, if we purposely commission ourselves to obey God and His word we will realize the results that He intended for His children. Those results would always be good!

It is very important that we examine what we believe and then follow through with those beliefs to God's desired result. Often we confess that we know or believe certain things from God's word, but we fail to carry through to completion.

In Finis Dake's book *Power over Sickness and Disease[3]*, Dake shares the following:

*In Isaiah 45:7 we read, "I create evil." The Hebrew word for "evil" is ra, meaning*

---

[2] Commission = 1 : a warrant granting certain powers and imposing certain duties 2 : a certificate conferring military rank and authority 3 : authority to act as agent for another; also : something to be done by an agent 4 : a body of persons charged with performing a duty 5 : the doing of some act; also : the thing done 6 : the allowance made to an agent for transacting business for another

[3] http://yourlastresort.net/index.cfm?PageID=5713

2

*"adversity," "affliction," "calamity," "grief," "misery," "sorrow," "wretchedness," "trouble," "harm," "distress," "ill," and "mischief." These things are the harvest of sowing and breaking the laws of God. This is a law fixed by God, and it cannot be altered or changed.* **If any free moral agent chooses to break laws, contrary to his creative makeup and the highest good of his being and of the universe, he must pay the penalty of reaping what he has sown.**

*When the Bible says that God puts physical sickness and disease upon men, as in the following Scriptures, it simply means that His law of sowing and reaping is being executed by the proper agencies to enforce this law (Exod. 15:26; Deut. 7:15; 28:1-68). In these passages it is stated that sickness is the result of sowing sin. If there had been no sin there would have been no disease. In many places where it speaks of God taking a certain action, in reality He used proper agents actually to bring it to pass. It is said that God sent Joseph into Egypt, but in reality his brethren were the ones who sold him to the Ishmaelites (Gen. 45:4-8). It is said that God would visit Israel and lead them out of Egypt, but in reality God used Moses and Aaron as his agents to do this (Gen. 50:24; Ps. 77:20). It is said on numerous occasions that God subdued Israel's enemies, but in reality He used human agency to do it (Judg. 4:14-23). The same is true of the law of sickness and disease. He has given the actual power of this law into the hands of demon powers.*

*MAN THE LAW-BREAKER. Man is the great law-breaker, and he must reap what he sows. Man is responsible in the first place for yielding to sin and Satan and submitting to demon powers that take advantage of his sinful state and cause all kinds of failures and sufferings in his life. He is responsible for breaking God's laws; for living in lusts and uncleanness, which breeds sickness and disease; for accidents due to careless living; for lack of power from God to defeat Satan; for lack of proper exercise; for failure to keep the body in a clean, healthy state; for overwork and intemperance in eating, in drinking, and in proper care of the body; for the wrong use of his faculties, which cause worry and fear that tear down natural and spiritual resistance to sickness; for certain conditions that pass on from one generation to another; and for failure to appropriate the benefits for which Jesus died so that he can be healed and delivered from satanic powers. Sins of all kinds, rebellion, and misuse of the tongue, hardness of heart, fleshly lusts, pride, unbelief, and many other personal acts on the part of men have caused them to break the laws of God and give the agents of sin, sickness, and death the opportunity to bring about sickness in their lives. This vulnerability does not mean that demons always take advantage at once, for sometimes it is to their advantage not to use their powers to bring sickness upon the law-breakers. But eventually those who sow will have to reap.*

We can see then that whatever we permit into our lives, whether through commission or omission, we reap the results. It is vitally important for us to carry through with what we believe from God's word and reap God's best. If we know what is good, but fail to carry on to obedience, we could reap sins results and end up attaching ourselves to demons and their dark deeds.

There are examples of this.

## Examples

*A mountain:* Jesus told His disciples that if they would believe and not doubt they would see results.[4] Their faith, obviously, would be based upon what they believed. If their belief was faulty they would not realize the desired results of what they asked for or commanded in spiritual realms.

It must be noted here, that before the disciples could see the mountain cast into the sea in the natural realm they first must believe

---

[4] Matthew 21:21 Jesus replied, "I tell you the truth, if you have faith and do not doubt, not only can you do what was done to the fig tree, but also you can say to this mountain, 'Go, throw yourself into the sea,' and it will be done. 22 If you believe, you will receive whatever you ask for in prayer."

that it was possible based upon spiritual truths from God's word and will.

**Wisdom:** James the Apostle tells us that our request of God most be founded upon solid belief and no doubts.[5] This belief must refrain from any double-mindedness. Double-mindedness, as mentioned before with commission, must remain solidly on what God has said and promised; there is no room for duplicity.

Also, wisdom will not be given to the person who is double-minded and unstable[6]. Those people who are unstable and lacking control claim some truths but will compromise for many different reasons which often nullifies faith. I will discuss this in a later chapter.

**Obedience:** [7] Disobedience puts a person in the realm of Satan, who was the first rebel.

---

[5] James 1:6 But when he asks, he must believe and not doubt, because he who doubts is like a wave of the sea, blown and tossed by the wind. 7 That man should not think he will receive anything from the Lord; 8 he is a double-minded man, unstable in all he does.
[6] FICKLE : VACILLATING;   also    : lacking effective emotional control
[7] Romans 2:6 God "will give to each person according to what he has done." 7 To those who by persistence in doing good seek glory, honor and immortality, he will give eternal life. 8 But for those who are self-

Rebellion is the deliberate choice to disregard God's will. Rebellion usually comes as a result of a person seeking self-gratification and disregarding the consequence. Once we know this truth it is so very important that we carry through with persistent action and choices.

Our persistence must totally deny anything that is contrary to God's will and word. We must have an attitude that demands holiness, righteousness, and purity. We must demand that we refuse evil in any form, no matter how subtle or benign it may appear.

I have found that most Christians give into weaknesses, faults, and anti-God associations because they refuse to see that there must be a disconnect from the world and all its trappings of darkness. These trappings take on many forms and usually are very subtle.

A good rule to follow would be a rule that would require us to walk in any truth that God makes known to us. Even if those truths go

---

seeking and who reject the truth and follow evil, there will be wrath and anger.

against some long held ideas, beliefs, celebrations, or practices.

We can see then, that our belief system makes all the difference on how we walk out our Christianity. If we fail to put the proper importance to God's word and the efficacy inherent in it, we will fail to realize many other things that can make us victorious and accomplish much for the Lord.

Everything we believe or fail to believe, or mix with any falsehoods of darkness, makes up our total belief system. That belief system drives our heart (soul or center) and causes us to accept or deny the promises of God.[8]

Our beliefs must not have any room for careless words or the acceptance of anything that is not of God or that comes from the world. If we do not guard what we believe we may

---

[8] Matt 12:33 "Make a tree good and its fruit will be good, or make a tree bad and its fruit will be bad, for a tree is recognized by its fruit. 34 You brood of vipers, how can you who are evil say anything good? For out of the overflow of the heart the mouth speaks. 35 The good man brings good things out of the good stored up in him, and the evil man brings evil things out of the evil stored up in him. 36 But I tell you that men will have to give account on the day of judgment for every careless word they have spoken. 37 For by your words you will be acquitted, and by your words you will be condemned."

accept things that can destroy our faith and cause us to question God's power and promises.

# 2

# Ignorance

Someone once said that ignorance is bliss. I'm not sure if ignorance is bliss, but I do know that ignorance can be deadly.

In the Old Testament God addressed the question of ignorance and graphically commanded what must be done. God's stance against sins committed in ignorance and those committed willfully was basically the same. He did make a way when someone sinned in ignorance to be forgiven and reconciled, but did not diminish the wickedness of the sin. Sin separates humans from God and ignorance is no excuse once a person is informed of it.

***Numbers 15:27 And if any soul sin through ignorance, then he shall bring a she goat of the first year for a sin offering.28 And the priest shall make an atonement for the soul that sinneth ignorantly, when he sinneth by ignorance before the Lord, to make an atonement for him; and it shall be forgiven him. 29 Ye shall have one law for him that sinneth through ignorance, both for him that is born among the children of Israel, and for the stranger that sojourneth among them. 30 But the soul that doeth ought presumptuously, whether he be born in the land, or a stranger, the same reproacheth the Lord; and that soul shall be cut off from among his people. 31 Because he hath despised the word of the Lord, and hath broken his commandment, that soul shall utterly be cut off; his iniquity shall be upon him.*** KJV

Someone once said, *I guess God still blesses us in our ignorance.* I'm not sure that is correct. If God sees sins committed in ignorance and those committed in rebellion as the same then He can't bless those who sin.

Now I know what someone will say, *What about the verse that states, "He lets the rain fall on the just as well as the unjust?"* Trying to use that verse to prove that ignorance is an excuse to sin is ridiculous at best. Yes, God does let the rain fall on the just and the unjust, but once either is given the truth they are no longer ignorant.

Once a person is given the truth and they acknowledge it they then stand under the law which either condemns or acquits the sinner. This reality is brought out very well in Numbers 15: 30 ***But the soul that doeth ought presumptuously, whether he be born in the land, or a stranger, the same reproacheth the Lord; and that soul shall be cut off from among his people. 31 <u>Because he hath despised the word of the Lord, and hath broken his commandment</u>, that soul shall utterly be cut off; his iniquity shall be upon him. KJV*** (underline added)

When a person comes to the Lord and claims to be a son or daughter of God, through Jesus, they then stand in a different spiritual position then they did before.

***Ephesians 4:17 So I tell you this, and insist on it in the Lord, that you must no longer***

*live as the Gentiles do, in the futility (ignorance) of their thinking. 18 They are darkened in their understanding and separated from the life of God because of the ignorance that is in them due to the hardening of their hearts.*

Their new spiritual position is to be walking in the life of God. In that life there is freedom, joy, peace, healing, needs being met, and provision provided for. If we continue to live out those things we know are wrong we are no longer in ignorance, but only rebellion. That rebellion then will nullify the blessings that God would desire for us.

Jesus spoke of the willful ignorance that we can fall prey to when He came to Jerusalem. Matthew 23:37 *"O Jerusalem, Jerusalem, you who kill the prophets and stone those sent to you, how often I have longed to gather your children together, as a hen gathers her chicks under her wings, but you were not willing. 38 Look, your house is left to you desolate. 39 For I tell you, you will not see me again until you say, 'Blessed is he who comes in the name of the Lord.'"*

The *"but you were not willing"* statement was spoken to a nation and city that refused the truth even when it was standing in their presence. God wanted to give greater blessing to His people and special city but they were trying to live in two realms. One realm was the realm of legalism and the other was the realm of false repentance. Legalism demanded the adherence to many man made laws while false repentance approached God without obedience.

You see, we think that God will bless us in our ignorance, all the while we know truth, but continue in our disobedience. God wants to bless but He can't release the best because we try to live in two realms. Ignorance doesn't even play a role as we claim to be Christians and have been given the truth.

We all too often miss God's blessings because we try to live our Christianity in the two realms mentioned above. We unwittingly go along with things that have to do with spiritual darkness, or border on spiritual darkness, all the while seeking blessings from God but failing to see much of it being materialized in our life.

I believe we don't see all that God has for us because we permit false gods to live among us. I don't necessarily believe we willfully worship or accept false gods, but I do believe we go along with many things that false gods are attached to or originate with false gods and the things of spiritual darkness.

It must be understood that demons attach themselves to anything that has to do with false worship, idols, and gods or goddess in any form. It is those demons that cause much sickness and abnormalities in body, soul, and spirit. Often people will not realize freedom until they rid themselves of the object, spiritual power or ungodly association, and then repent and turn to God.

God asks the question *"**What communion hath light with darkness?**"* We must know how to answer the question and then follow through with proper and decisive action.

# 3

# The gods Among Us

If I would claim that many Christians worship false gods, I'm sure I would have an argument on my hands. If I would claim that many Christians willfully rebel against God, I would probably have less of an argument. If I would claim that we tend to pick and choose which truths of God's word we accept and then live, I'm sure I would not have much of an argument as most of us know that we tend to do this. But, as God's children, shouldn't we walk in the truths that we are informed of? I say yes we should, and must, for our own well-being!

I'm afraid that we miss out on many of the blessings that God wants to bring us because we have associations with false gods that are among us.

I know that that statement is drastic and shocking. I know that we would want to argue the point and probably use the ignorance card to make our point. But, before you throw this book away, please give me more time and pages to help you understand where I'm coming from.

## The gods among us

I want to make something very clear in this section. When I talk about the gods among us, I am putting anything that is contrary to God's will and biblically stated ways in the same category. I have come to realize that humans align themselves with either God's power or the powers of darkness. The powers of darkness obviously are in Satan's realm and he is the author of anything that pulls mankind away from biblical truth and God's commands.

If I would ask you, *"Do you check out a horoscope? What is your Zodiac sign? Do you believe in luck? Do you check out astrology? What about the rabbit's foot or the horse shoe, do you think they help in any way? Do you believe Jesus is the only way to God the Father or is there another way? Do you believe in numerology or ever use the Ouija board?"*

Let's look at just one example of permitting false gods or the belief in those things that are against God's word. Let's take astrology;

After the warning against adding anything to God's Word in Deuteronomy 4:2, the Lord adds this: ***"And take heed, lest you lift your eyes to heaven, and when you see the sun, the moon, and the stars, all the host of heaven, you feel driven to worship them and serve them, which the Lord your God has given to all the peoples under the whole heaven as a heritage*** (4:19)." The word translated "serve" in that verse means "to be subject to." (You make yourself subject to the stars when you follow them or believe in them or seek them for guidance.)

God expressly forbids astrology, which is a form of interpreting omens, and places it in the same category as witchcraft and child sacrifice (Deuteronomy 18:10-14). He does not want us to place ourselves in spiritual and moral subjection to the stars and planets, but to Scripture alone. Anyone who claims to be a Christian but also studies his horoscope is denying the authority of God's Word, and following a false and spiritually deadly authority — that of Satan himself.

God specifically identified astrologers as among those who will experience the fire of His judgment: *You are wearied in the multitude of your counsels; let now the astrologers, the stargazers, and the monthly prognosticators stand up and save you from what shall come upon you. Behold, they shall be as stubble, the fire shall burn them; they shall not deliver themselves from the power of the flame; it shall not be a coal to be warmed by, nor a fire to sit before!* (Isaiah 47:13-14)

Virtually every pagan religion, both ancient and modern (including Buddhism and

Hinduism today) involves some form of astrology using the Zodiac.

I believe many people have associations with false gods by giving false gods an innocent, but permissible right into their lives. An example would be the daily checking of horoscopes.

Now, before I go on, please bear with me, and have an open, but prayerful heart and mind.

Most Christians celebrate Easter. This holiday celebrates Jesus' resurrection. Easter is the name of a false goddess and most of the Easter celebration is directly associated with this false goddess. Even its name comes from the goddess Astrate.

God tells us in Exodus 23:*13* *"**Be careful to do everything I have said to you. Do not invoke the names of other gods; do not let them be heard on your lips.**"* Easter has a false goddess name, and the eggs, bunnies, forty days of fasting, sunrise services, and the like all come from this false god. I address this false goddess in my book *Easter – Not What You Think.*

When a person celebrates the Resurrection and uses the name Easter, permits the eggs, bunnies and the pagan trappings of Easter, a person is giving a false goddess credence, whether they believe it or not. God forbids it even in ignorance! I believe we should celebrate the Resurrection, but we must not call it Easter.

## Luck

God tells us that our time on this earth should be directed by Him. He speaks to us in His word, Holy Scripture, and informs us that if we will acknowledge Him and His ways He will direct our steps. *"The steps of a good man are ordered by the Lord: and he delighteth in his way. Though he fall, he shall not be utterly cast down: for the Lord upholdeth him with his hand."* Psalms 37:23-24 KJV.

We can see that God gives no room for luck or happenstance, either a person lets God direct his steps or he doesn't. If he doesn't then he is at the mercy of the world, weather, and the corrupted wisdom of man.

Luck is not an inexplicable force that cannot be understood, explained, or accounted for.

It is certainly true that there are many things that are not understood in life, but luck is not one of them. The superstitious beliefs that are taught about a "luck-force" existing beyond human knowledge and comprehension add up to nothing more than groundless, off-beat speculation. The natural-minded, irrational man has imagined the existence of a force called luck, and then says, "It can't be explained." So the non-existent, but popular imagined force of luck has developed into a catchall explanation for good and evil. But, the only forthright and truthful explanation for the forces of good and evil are clearly spelled out in God's Word. There are no other spiritual forces affecting our lives, beyond those that are thoroughly explained by God's Word.

Luck is not an innocent, harmless, crutch-word that can be used without any real impact or consequences. It is not a harmless activity to contradict God and the truth of His Word. God promises in His Word that He is the legitimate and genuine bestower of blessings and benefits, and that true prosperity comes by Him alone.

By using the so-called lucky items, such as the rabbit's foot, horse shoes, lucky stars, astrology, numerology, and the horoscope is seeking direction and protection outside of God.

When a Christian uses the above mentioned items or has a luck directed attitude they are trying to seek direction from sources other than God. When the Christian does this he/she is opening themselves up to the influences of demons and Satan. In this duplicitous state God cannot bless or give guidance because He refuses to allow darkness and light to co-mingle.

## Mediums

It always amazes me when I hear of someone consulting a medium, fortune teller, or psychic. I know of Christians that do this and can't understand that what they are doing is in direct rebellion to God and His word. *"'Do not turn to mediums or seek out spiritists, for you will be defiled by them. I am the Lord your God.* Leviticus 19:31. Being defiled by this association can cause sickness and poverty in many forms.

The people who seek mediums, fortune tellers, or psychics are placing themselves under the demon that controls those individuals. The medium may deny any association with demons, but in their ignorance they are being controlled never-the-less.

I'm sure you have seen the well-known T.V. mediums and seers who claim to speak to the dead or are being led by the dead. Many of these misguided individuals even believe they are being led by God. They sound nice, comforting, and convincing, but believe me, they are being fooled and only defiled, along with those who seek out their services.

When a Christian seeks out any guidance, other than Godly guidance, they are opening themselves up to doctrines of demons.

*Now the Spirit speaketh expressly, that in the latter times some shall depart from the faith, giving heed to seducing spirits, and doctrines of devils; Speaking lies in hypocrisy; having their conscience seared with a hot iron;* 1 Timothy 4:1-2 KJV

# Ouija board[9]

The Ouija board has been used, or maybe I should say, played with by many people throughout the world. This supposedly innocent game played with one, two or more people has brought laughs and giggles to unsuspecting seekers.

It too has its foundation in the realm of demons and was used as a means of ostensibly contacting the dead and the spirit-world.

I personally know of relatives and friends who have constantly used the Ouija board to seek guidance for their lives.

---

[9] Chao Wei-pang. 1942. "The origin and Growth of the Fu Chi", Folklore Studies 1:9–27 "One of the first mentions of the automatic writing method used in the Ouija board is found in China around 1100 AD, in historical documents of the Song Dynasty. The method was known as "planchette writing". The use of planchette writing as a means of ostensibly contacting the dead and the spirit-world continued, and, albeit under special rituals and supervisions, was a central practice of the Quanzhen School, until it was forbidden by the Qing Dynasty.[9] Several entire scriptures of the Daozang are supposedly works of automatic planchette writing. Similar methods of mediumistic spirit writing have been widely practiced in ancient India, Greece, Rome, and medieval Europe."

I know of a woman and her daughter who used the Ouija board often and even saw a form of another being in their mirror which they called their spiritual guide. This woman and her daughter had constant sicknesses and in the mother's case died young. Both of these woman confessed that they were Christian, but they never seemed to be free from strange sickness or mental confusion.

## Idols we permit

We can permit, often in ignorance, false gods to live among us in the form of figurines. You know the type; the fat little Buddha that is bought on a trip someplace, the slim Indian god that is oh so cute, the sign of the Zodiac above the door or hanging on the wall, the horse shoe on the door, the lucky charm, or the pretty silver Egyptian Ankh that is worn around one's neck[10].

All of the above mentioned items have to do with false gods and have their origin in the

---

[10] ☥ The ankh appears frequently in Egyptian tomb paintings and other art, often at the fingertips of a god or goddess in images that represent the deities of the afterlife conferring the gift of life on the dead person's mummy.

powers of darkness. These items are in direct conflict with Christian principles and a proper walk with God. They represent a form of belief or trust in the god or goddess they represent, either overtly or covertly. And when found within one's home gives permission for demons to come in. They are in direct conflict with God's command not to have them in one's home or on one's person.

I have often ministered to families who had problems with sickness, poverty, and some sort of mental confusion, but could not find freedom. While ministering to these families I have found they owned and displayed a figurine of Buddha, Indian god, or other such statue. After sharing with these families of the dangers of possessing a representation of a false god they destroyed the item. Almost instantly these families found freedom and release.

The above mentioned families were Christian confessing families and did not understand the dangers that are associated with false gods. They, like many, had the items in ignorance or saw them as cute little figurines. This should be a good lesson to us all!

# 4

## Total Freedom Demands Oneness

As I have discussed earlier, we must walk out our life with God in a *one-realm-reality*. What I mean by a *one-realm-reality* is that we must not permit anything into our life that has to do with the realm of Satan, demons, or false religions and their gods.

I have met Christians who have told me many frustrating stories of not realizing freedom in their lives, but claim to love the Lord, follow His instructions, and walk the best way they know how.

Before we go further, we need to understand a very foundational truth. Always remember, God is not the problem, His word is always correct, and His ways to walk with Him are set in spiritual cement. God does not vary in His love, fairness, and commands. He means what He says and requires our utmost obedience and love.

One of the founding realities of a proper walk with God is a zeroing in on seeking Him above all else. *But seek first his kingdom and his righteousness, and all these things will be given to you as well.* Matthew 6:33-34

The seeking first principle must deny anything, let me repeat, anything, that denies God, refuses to trust Him, or comes from the darker elements of life and the wrong spirit realm. Any of those things mentioned in the previous chapter are of the wrong spiritual realm.

We tie God's hands when we permit anything of Satan, those things of spiritual dark nature, or out-right rebellion to His word and commands.

If we fail to obey God and find sickness, confusion, or lack in our life we should pretty well know that we have failed to obey God or have let something into our lives that is not of God. However, He is such a gentleman and will not force us to give up those things we demand to be more important than Him. It is our choice!

Often I have ministered to people who have had in their homes the items mentioned in chapter three, but could not be healed, set free, or find rest until they repented and discarded the items.

I have ministered to many people who seemingly have done all the proper spiritual things, according to scripture, but still lack healing or freedom.

After careful and personal research I found that the one thing that made the difference in their freedom was their association with items, beliefs or actions that were contrary to God and His will and ways.

God is a jealous[11] being. God is not a jealous being as we are, but a jealous being that will not permit the enemy of our souls to co-mingle with us. His jealousy is a protective form of jealousy.

*"You shall not make for yourself an idol in the form of anything in heaven above or on the earth beneath or in the waters below. 5 You shall not bow down to them or worship them; for I, the Lord your God, am a jealous God, punishing the children for the sin of the fathers to the third and fourth generation of those who hate me, 6 but showing love to a thousand [generations] of those who love me and keep my commandments.* Exodus 20:4

Since God is a being who will not share His love for His children with powers of darkness, He also will not force His children to walk with Him. Their desire must come from free-will, but they must understand that with free-will comes responsibility.

If a Christian permits the items and celebrations mentioned above, God will step back and let them witness, realize, and benefit

---

[11] Jealous - 1 : demanding complete devotion, 2 : suspicious of a rival or of one believed to enjoy an advantage, 3 : VIGILANT

from their association with darkness. God would still love the child, but they would not realize the full benefits as one of His children. They must break off any association with idols, false gods, or the practices that are contrary to God's will and ways.

## Knowledge brings freedom

**My people are destroyed for lack of knowledge: because thou hast rejected knowledge, I will also reject thee,** Hosea 4:66 KJV.

When we realize truth we have responsibility for that truth. We can't say we don't have the knowledge to be free and capable of realizing God's best once we know the truth. It is the very truth and understanding that God wants His children to be free from any associations with demons, Satan, and the powers of darkness that separates true believers from those who will not submit to truth. If we confess Jesus and profess to believe God's word, we then are responsible to walk in all aspects of His word.

We cannot associate ourselves with the Zodiac, the name Easter (this is a false goddess), Astrology, Numerology, Buddha, Rabbit's Foot, Krishna, Charms, Ouija board, Palm readers, daily Horoscope, or Mediums and walk in the fullness of God and the freedom He desires for His children. There are consequences with those associations and it is always bad. Those associations bring sickness, infirmity, loss, poverty, and death in all forms.

Repentance is required!

*Repent! Turn away from all your offenses; then sin will not be your downfall. 31 Rid yourselves of all the offenses you have committed, and get a new heart and a new spirit. Why will you die, O house of Israel? 32 For I take no pleasure in the death of anyone, declares the Sovereign Lord. Repent and live!* Ezekiel 18:30-32.

Once we accept the truth and repent God promises to restore and heal. What we do with the truth given in this book can be a liberating reality or it can become a curse to us.

Scripture informs us that a curse cannot come to those who walk with God, but if we refuse God and His word a curse could come to us. The willful act of denying truth would be a reason for a curse to come.

**Like a fluttering sparrow or a darting swallow, an undeserved curse does not come to rest.** Proverbs 26:2

The curse would be self-imposed because one would refuse the truth. God would not bring the curse, but the refusal of God's word would give Satan and his demons permission to come into one's life and bring chaos.

**What will you do with this truth?**